GLEAMS FROM THE RAWDAT AL-SHUHADA'

لمعات من
روضة الشهداء
على أصُول القلادنة

Gleams from the
RAWDAT
AL-SHUHADA'
(Garden of the Martyrs)
of Husayn Vaiz Kashifi

PREPARED FOR ENGLISH RECITAL
BY ABDAL HAKIM MURAD

MUSLIM ACADEMIC TRUST

The Muslim Academic Trust
14 St Paul's Road
Cambridge CB1 2EZ
United Kingdom

ISBN: 978 1 902350 11 0
www.britishmuslimsong.co.uk

PRINTED IN TURKEY

Contents

Introduction

KAMAL AL-DIN HUSAYN Va'iz Kashifi (d. 910 AH) was one of the most brilliant literary figures and religious scholars of the final flourishing of the rule of the Timurid dynasty in Central Asia. Originally from Sabzavar he came to Herat after seeing a dream of Sa'd al-Din Kashgari, a saintly disciple of Baha' al-Din Naqshband, founder of the Sufi order of that name. Although Kashgari died before his arrival, Kashifi chose to associate with the city's Naqshbandi circles, a decision which did much to shape his later literary output. He became close to Abd al-Rahman Jami (817-898 AH), sometimes described as the last great Persian poet, who was himself deeply embedded in Naqshbandi spiritual lore and technique, and who gave Kashifi his daughter in marriage. He also befriended the great poet and statesman Ali Shir Nevai, a great patron of the Naqshbandis, who appointed him Friday preacher at the city's main mosque. The connection was underlined when Kashifi's son Fakhr al-Din Ali had the distinction of composing the best-known biographical dictionary of Naqshbandi saints, the *Rashahat Ayn al-Hayat* (translated into English by the late Muhtar Holland as *Beads of Dew from the Source of Life*).

Kashifi's prolific literary output closely reflected his chosen Naqshbandi environment. His Qur'anic commentaries, of which the shortest, the *Mawahib-i Aliyya,* gained widespread respect among the Hanafi learned classes of India, combine literary and Sufi interests with a rigorous attachment to classical interpretative patterns. Another work, the *Akhlaq-i Muhsini*, is often regarded as the third great Persian work on ethics. Often imitated by later authors, it is divided into 40 chapters, each treating of a different virtue. Even better known was his *Anwar-i Suhayli*, the '*Lights of Canopus*', a highly-wrought expansion of the fables of *Kalila wa-Dimna* which had been grafted onto Islamic literature from India centuries before. Described by many in premodern times as the finest prose work ever compiled in the Persian language, it was for many years a required text for the examinations for the Indian civil service during British rule, being published first in Hertford as early as 1805. A further work of note is a long commentary, entitled *al-Risala al-Aliyya,* on forty selected hadith, in which a wide range of anecdotes and sayings are reported from the Companions, the Four Caliphs, Juwayni, Ibn Hanbal, Shafi'i and Abu Hanifa (the founder of Kashifi's own school).

The *Rawdat al-Shuhada'* (*Garden of Martyrs*), compiled only two years before Kashifi's death, stands as a further monument of Farsi literature. Composed in a relatively straightforward style which eschews some of the more baroque flourishes of the belle-lettrist style, it continues much earlier traditions of compiling texts on the suffering of the Prophet's family, but incorporates a wider range of material than any major author had hitherto attempted. Qur'anic texts, hadiths from the canonical collections, sayings of the early Muslims, and a range of other sources are woven together with works by several of Kashifi's contemporaries. He quotes a good deal from the *Rawdat al-ahbab,* a work on Prophetic biography by Jamal Husayni (d.927 AH), a leading preacher and Hanafi jurist of his city.

His debt to Jami, who had himself written more briefly on the tragedy which met al-Husayn on the field of Karbala, is especially evident. He frequently draws on Jami's *Shawahid al-Nubuwwa* (*Prophetic Testimonies*), a classic Naqshbandi text on *futuwwa,* the 'spiritual chivalry' whereby the initiate overcomes enemies in the soul and in the world while maintaining an ethos of courtesy and good manners. In fact we can perhaps see the *Rawda* as an expansive meditation on the theme of spiritual chivalry as pursued by the Naqshbandi authors of his tradition. This might explain the ongoing popularity of the work in the Ottoman world with its strong martial and mystical traditions, and where the poet Fuzuli produced a remarkable Turkish translation, the *Hadiqat al-Su'ada* (*Garden of the Fortunate),* a hugely-esteemed favourite among sultans, soldiers and scholars alike. The *Rawda,* along with the *Maqtal-i Husayn* (*Death of Husayn*) of the Naqshbandi master of Bursa Bahşioğlu Yahya, flowed into an entire genre of Ottoman literature, some of which is still read and recited to this day. The *Rawda* has also been hugely popular in Iran, India, and Central Asia.

The present booklet and the accompanying recording do not claim to be a translation of the text. Instead the intention has been to allow the traditional practice of commemorating the Prophetic House to find a voice, however tremulous and exploratory, in English. The chapter sequence of Kashifi's work has been maintained, and many of the individual songs which we include are distillations of the key themes of those chapters, and sometimes quote from them directly. But in line with the Protean spirit of a tradition which is always growing and adapting organically, we have been eclectic in including samples of other material. Hence we offer a translation of the celebrated ode in praise of Fatima by Mehmet Esad Erbili, the Naqshbandi shaykh and martyr of Turkey (d. 1930 CE). Lines from well-known poems by Mu'in al-Din Chishti and Abdallah al-Haddad also make an appearance. We also offer some samples from the famous *Terkib-bend* of the Ottoman poet and newspaper editor Ziya Pasha (d. 1880 CE), for which we have made use of the archaising but still effective translation by E.J.W. Gibb.

How to recall in modern English the mellifluous and syncopated music of the original? Kashifi's voice and delivery were so celebrated that his mosque was 'dangerously overcrowded' with enthusiastic hearers; Nevai called him 'the David of our times', recalling the golden voice of the ancient psalmist. For our simple, short and distant twenty-first century echo we have opted for some tunes from the Celtic fringe, so rich with its own tradition of lamentation. Whether the juxtaposition of the two worlds is effective we leave it to the listener to judge. But this is a first experiment, or a *tawaf al-qudum*; we leave it to future and greater talents to take this idea forward, and find a fitting way of incorporating Kashifi's timeless work in the emerging canon of British Muslim literature and culture.

Wa-bi'Llahi 't-tawfiq

ABDAL HAKIM MURAD

Ziya Pasha, *Terkib-bend*, First Extract

TR. E.J.W. GIBB

(*Spoken*:)

How passing strange a school this workshop of creation shows!
Its every fabric doth some script of the unknown expose.
The whirling heaven is a mill whose yield is agony;
Bewildered man is e'en the grain it grinds the while it goes.
Like to a demon fierce and fell its offspring it devours
How strange a nest doth this old hostelry of earth disclose!
If one should heedful scan the shows of all existent things,
Behold a dream, a fantasy, a tale of joys and woes.
All things soever in the world are borne towards an end;
Spring into autumn glides, and summer's heat to winter's snows.
It seems that man will never win Eternal Truth unto;
For logic and false reason seem to reason vague and futile shows.
O wherefore, Lord, is all this bitter stress and strife of pain,
The while a crust of bread is all the need man really knows?
There is no buckler underneath yon dome of turquoise hue;
Each atom is the goal 'gainst which fierce Fate his arrows throws.
The scheme of the Everlasting Will is working out its end;
But means are all the seeming good and ill that e'er arose.
All things existent are the workings of that mighty Power;
No circlings of blind Heaven's wheel, no tricks of Fortune, those.

CHAPTER ONE

The Tribulations of the Prophets

Ziya Paşa, *Terkib-bend*, Second Extract

TR. E.J.W. GIBB WITH AMENDMENTS

The Father of Mankind was cast from Eden's happy plain;
As place of trial for Abraham his offspring's neck was ta'en;
The grief of separation from his son was Jacob's bane.

The saintly Yusuf's biding-place was e'en the gaol and chain;
Ailments and aches of frame and limb Ayyub made groan in woeful vein;
And Zakariyya to the saw must needs his head constrain.

The Prophet Yahya was beheaded by fell tyranny;
Isa the Fatherless endured full much of grief and pain;
At Ta'if were the Prophet's legs to ruby turned, and then

Yon lustrous pearls were on the Day of Uhud broke atwain;
For hunger's pangs he bound the stone fast to his blessed waist amain,
Full little recked the Lord of Humankind of worldly gain.

The Blessed Haydar sank at last beneath the blade profane;
And Hasan, poisoned, passed away to Paradise the pure domain;
And foully murdered was the Monarch of the martyr-train.

In whomsoe'er the love of the Divine doth all ordain,
To him in that same fashion anguish and woe they still pertain,
To him in that same fashion woe and anguish still pertain.

(Chorus)

Salli rabbi ala'l-nabi amin il-alamayn
muballighi'r-risala, rafa'a qadra'l-haramayn
Salli rabbi wa-sallim ala jaddi'l-hasanayn

3

Prayer for the Day of Ashura

دعاء يوم عاشوراء

يَا قَابِلَ تَوْبَةِ آدَمَ يَوْمَ عَاشُورَاءَ ، يَا فَارِجَ كَرْبِ ذِي النُّونِ يَوْمَ عَاشُورَاءَ ،

يَا جَامِعَ شَمْلِ يَعْقُوبَ يَوْمَ عَاشُورَاءَ ، يَا سَامِعَ دَعْوَةِ مُوسَى وَهَارُونَ يَوْمَ

عَاشُورَاءَ ، يَا مُغِيثَ إِبْرَاهِيمَ مِنَ النَّارِ يَوْمَ عَاشُورَاءَ ، يَا رَافِعَ إِدْرِيسَ إِلَى

السَّمَاءِ يَوْمَ عَاشُورَاءَ ، يَا مُجِيبَ دَعْوَةِ صَالِحٍ فِي النَّاقَةِ يَوْمَ عَاشُورَاءَ ، يَا

نَاصِرَ سَيِّدِنَا مُحَمَّدٍ صَلَّى اللهُ عَلَيْهِ وَسَلَّمَ يَوْمَ عَاشُورَاءَ ، يَارَحْمَانَ الدُّنْيَا

وَالآخِرَةِ وَرَحِيمَهُمَا ، صَلِّ عَلَى سَيِّدِنَا مُحَمَّدٍ وَعَلَى آلِ سَيِّدِنَا مُحَمَّدٍ وَصَلِّ

عَلَى جَمِيعِ الأَنْبِيَاءِ وَالْمُرْسَلِينَ ، وَاقْضِ حَاجَاتِنَا فِي الدُّنْيَا وَالآخِرَةِ وَأَطِلْ

عُمْرَنَا فِي طَاعَتِكَ وَمَحَبَّتِكَ وَرِضَاكَ وَأَحْيِنَا حَيَاةً طَيِّبَةً وَتَوَفَّنَا عَلَى الإِيمَانِ

والإِسلامِ بِرَحْمَتِكَ يَا أَرْحَمَ الرَّاحِمِينَ

CHAPTER TWO

Quraysh Persecute the Master of Goodness

Ziya Paşa, *Terkib-bend*, Third Extract

The lion's cruel fangs do rend the screaming fawn their prey in twain.
The fierce and ravening wolf devours innocent sheep in gule and pain,
The fierce and ravening wolf devours the sheep in gule and pain.

E'en so the royal falcon hath the harmless pigeon slain,
The fish that swims the ocean turns to the fowl of heaven's gain;
The diver seeking pearls is sought by sharks in their domain.

Since e'er the world hath been the world this rule we see pertain:
Before the vilest scoundrel people of heart are humbled low.
The courted dullard lifts on high a brow without a brain.

Condemned and desperate the sage must ever humbly deign.
Fair fortune doth caress the fool, crowning his every hope of gain,
While for its song the nightingale imprisoned pines in vain.

(Chorus)

Salli rabbi ala'l-nabi amin il-alamayn
muballighi'r-risala, rafa'a qadra'l-haramayn
Salli rabbi wa-sallim ala jaddi'l-hasanayn

Litany XX

Tune: Manx traditional

Baritone

Sal - li rab - bi 'a - la'n - na - bi sha - fi - 'i - na Ah - mad   Ka'l - ghay - thi fi fa -

Bar.

la - tin ja - 'a - na bi'l - ma - dad   wa - aa - lu - hu'l - mu - kar - ra - mu fi   kul - li ba -

Bar.

lad   Shi - fa' - un li'l - qal - bi's - sa - qim maw - la - na Mu - ham - mad

صَلِّ رَبِّ عَلَى النَّبِي شَفِيعِنَا أَحْمَد

كَالغَيْثِ فِي فَلَاةٍ جَاءَنَا بِالمَدَد

وَآلُهُ المُكَرَّمُ فِي كُلِّ بَلَد

شِفَاءٌ لِلقَلْبِ السَّقِيم مَوْلَا نَا مُحَمَّد

6

CHAPTER THREE

Death of the Master of the Messengers

al-Wafât al-Nabawiyya

Tune: An Innis Aigh

All men upon this poor earth must die
Each soul that liveth twixt earth and sky
The angel heeds not the orphan's cry
And so did death take the prince of men.

Sick did he lie in his widow's house
His fever grave, nurséd by that spouse
The people silent around his house
And so did death take the prince of men.

The time is come, said that Prophet dear
But come to me and gather near
Ere I pass on, do my counsel hear
For soon must death take the prince of men.

In seven vessels from seven springs
In bringing water that good earth brings
They loved him more than all earthly things
But soon must death take the prince of men.

Said he, I choose the Exalted Friend
A peace and blessing that shall not end
I go ahead, you my way shall wend,
For soon must death take the prince of men.

Enshroud me in these clothes of mine
This woollen mantle of plain design
Let perfume please my Lord Divine
For soon must death take the prince of men.

They asked, And who'll lay you in your grave?
Said he: My family, bold and brave,
With angels who their hearts shall lave.
And so did death take the prince of men.

He bade his daughter to come so near
And then he whispered close in her ear
They saw her tears, and then her good cheer
And so did death take the prince of men.

Though loved he died, but we meet again
Amid the terrors of Judgement Plain
His intercession breaks our chain
Call grace and peace on the prince of men.

(Chorus)

Inna'n-niraana qad ukhmidat
wa'l-huru'l-'inu tazayyanat
Thumma al-mala'ikatu saffat
ila qudumi rasuli'Llah

CHAPTER 4

Fatima the Radiant

Istighfar 1

إِنَّ اللهَ غَفُورٌ رَحِيمٌ

وَكُلُّ الَّذِي دُونَ الفِرَاقِ قَلِيلُ   لِكُلِّ اجْتِمَاعٍ مِنْ خَلِيلَيْنِ فُرْقَةٌ

دَلِيلٌ عَلَى أَنْ لَا يَدُومَ خَلِيلُ   وَإِنَّ افْتِقَارِي فَاطِمًا بَعْدَ أَحْمَدٍ

Mother of Sorrows

Words: Esad Erbilli

Tune: Anach Cuain

Mother of Sorrows

Recall the father and mother pure
Perfect parents to every faithful heart
One day did think on the garden sure
Yearning, burning, all for that land apart.
Then came an angel with wondrous news
Falling like an apple from heaven's bower
The garden's Lord loved that couple fair
So Khadija brought forth that perfect flower.

In days of darkness the heathen cried
Let the moon be split by this chosen one!
With tongues like serpents they all denied
Open wide, their eyes could not see that sun.
Their scorn weighed hard on Khadija's heart
Ah, alas, cried she, to her holy spouse
But then her womb did good news impart
Fear not! God shall save servants of His House.

No other lady shall be her peer
God's own nature makes her the prophets' pride
The shining names of that daughter dear
Signalling the virtues of Ali's bride
The shining lady the chaste and pure
Mother of two sons, each a perfect guide,
The modest daughter, ever demure,
Queen of women who paradise abide.

Her noble father this word did say:
Fatima's a piece of my flesh, he said.
Whoso shall harm her doth God betray
So too doth he harm me, thus he said.
That child breathed deep of his perfume sweet
Like her soul his soul, in his steps she trod,
Water and bread ground from humble wheat
In the joy of faith did they serve their God.

So thirteen years ere the hijra was
Dwelt she humbly in her father's house
With many angels she served his cause
Filled the world with light as she served her spouse.
So hearer flee from the burning blaze
Seek forgiveness for all your evil days
Give prayers and blessings and always praise
She whom God did keep from all evil ways.

CHAPTER 5

Aspects of the Life of Imam Ali

⁘

Eulogy of Ali ibn Abi Talib

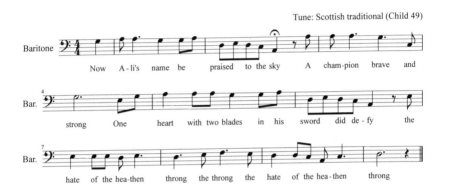

Now Ali's name be praised to the sky
A champion brave and strong
One heart with two blades in his sword did defy
The hate of the heathen throng, the throng
The hate of the heathen throng.

In the thirteenth spring of the Elephant's year
Did Abu Talib smile,
The Lion of God in this world did appear
Full free of pride and guile.

Then Providence placed him in Prophecy's house
As cousin to the chosen one,
When Gabriel came God's truth to announce
Straightway to that truth he won.

13

He married the light of God's chosen one
That Fatima al-Batul
Of worldly wealth he was owner of none
illa irth ar-Rasul.

At peace he lay in his holy teacher's place
Harun in Musa's stead,
A Yemeni robe veiled the sight of Quraysh
And thus his master sped.

At Uhud and Badr and Hunayn was he seen,
Where swords flashed like the sun,
The rallying cry from the hill and ravine
Was know that our God is One.

La fata illa Ali comes the cry
Alone see him slay Walid,
The champions of Khaybar thought to defy
His sabre but did concede.

The city of knowledge took him for its gate
Two guards stood watch each side,
Its towers watched by the road that is straight
Its master the seer guide.

No beggar heard rebuke at his door,
He worked the fields for a wage,
He gave his humble fare to the poor
He had nor serf nor page.

The treasures of Persia and Rome at his feet
His eye never glanced that way,
Instead of the palace of Kufa so sweet
He slept on sand and hay.

Ibn Tayyah came to call him for the Prayer
He reached the prayer hall gate,
Then Ibn Muljam, his blade in the air,
He slew him in bile and hate.

Thus while he lived, and also as he died,
He filled the world with signs.
All noble youth take Ali as their guide
His saintly courage shines.

(Chorus 1)

Ya Qabila 't-tawbi min khata'in
Ya wasi' al-ihsan
Akrim bi'l-aali dhawi sharafin
Hum manba' al-iman

(Chorus 2)

Ya rabb al-bayti wa'l-harami
Irhamna bi'l-Qur'an
Wa-ayyid sadatan ahla karami
Hum naslu Aliyyi al-Shan

CHAPTER 6

Virtues of Imam Hasan

Virtues of Imam Hasan

Tune: English Traditional (Child 93)

Ey   shur-bet - e   derd - e tu   da - va - ye dil a - shub - e ba - la - ye tu

a - ta - ye dil

Now call to your mind my companion in grief
Al-Hasan bin Ali the prince of belief

Al-Sibt and al-Sayyid, Mujtaba Taqi
Al-Zaki, the flower of prophecy's tree

His grandfather gave him, with Azra'il by,
the prayer for good fortune, face bright like the sky.

He prayed for the Garden and cried from the Fire,
He honoured the laws that the King did require.

The beggars would eat from the crusts on the street
From love did he join them, and with them did eat.

He saw the black slave servant feeding a hound
He bought him and freed him and so was renowned.

A treaty he made, that great hero of peace
The Muslims united from rancors released.

He dwelt in Medina the city of light
His home like a schoolhouse, in learning's delight.

He died in Medina, and there is his grave
Descendants aplenty to the Umma he gave.

So pray for his spirit and daughters and sons
That God resurrect us with those blessed ones.

(Chorus)

ay shurbat-e dard-e tu davā-ye dil
āshub-e balā-ye tu ʿaṭā-ye dil
az nāme-ye ḥamd-e tu shafā-ye dil
v'az nam-e ḥabīb-e tu ṣafā-ye dil

آشوب بلای تو عطـای دل   اي شربت درد تو دوای دل

واز نام حبیب تو صفای دل   از نامه حـــمد تو شفای دل

CHAPTER 7

Virtues of Imam Husayn

⁘

Shah-e man Husayn

Tune: English traditional

Shāh-e man Ḥusayno
dīn-e man Ḥusayno
Sare dad na dad dast
ḥaqqa ke binā-ye

pādshāh ast Ḥusayno
dīn-penāh Ḥusayno
dar dast-e Yazīdo
vaḥdet ast Ḥusayno

I.

See the light of dawn glow
For the second grandson
Feel the breeze of joy blow
Ahmad's sweetest loved one

God for us did bestow
Fatima his mother
Every blessing did show
Ali for his father

2.
In his blessed arms held
Mustafa his grandchild
Breathed his fragrance soft smelled
Blessed moments full whiled

Beauty in his name spelled
Fortune for our fortune
Seven years until quelled
By death's fell misfortune

3.
Ana min al-Ḥusayn
Spoke his blessed grandsire
Union that can't wane
Union ever higher

Ana min al-Ḥusayn
Wa'l-Ḥusaynu minni
Ana min al-Ḥusayn
Wa'l-Ḥusaynu minni

Istighfar 2

Tune: Scottish traditional

Baritone

As - tagh - fi - rul - Lah wa - a - tu - bu - i - layh as - tagh - fi - rul

Bar.

Lah wa - a - tu - bu - i - layh as - tagh - fi - rul - Lah wa - a - tu - bu - i -

Bar.

layh as - tagh - fi - rul - Lah wa - a - tu - bu - i - layh

Litany XXXIV

Tune: Irish traditional

Baritone

Sal - la-Llah a - la - Mu-ham - mad sal - la-Lah a - la - 'na - bi

Bar.

sal - la-Llah a - la - Mu-ham - mad sal - la Llah - a - la - 'na - bi

CHAPTER 8

The Martyrdom of Muslim b. Aqil

Song of the Kufan Braves

Tune: Fear a' Bhàta

نشيد جند الكوفة

Song of the Kufan Braves

في مَحَجَّةِ الجِهَادِ ثَوَابُ المَوْلَى لِلغُزَاةِ	أَيُّهَا المُجَاهِرُونَ بِالوَلَاءِ وَالصَّفَاءِ
جِئْنَا صَفًّا بَعْدَ صَفٍّ وَخَلْفَ رَايَاتِ الجَلَا	ثُمَّ جِئْنَا قَاصِدِينَ المَجْدَ فِي جُنْدِ الوَفَاءِ
لِلرِّمَاحِ وَالكِفَاحِ وَرَمْيِ السَّهْمِ لِلعِدَا	مَا لِلكُوفَةِ الكَرِيمَةِ الرَّفَّاضُ لِلفِدَاءِ
لِلقُلُوبِ فِي الحُرُوبِ نُورُ السِّنَانِ وَالسَّنَا	مِنْ مُطَاعٍ وَشُجَاعٍ اُنْظُرُوا إِلَى البَهَاءِ
كَالحَجِيجِ فِي الفِجَاجِ فِي يَوْمِ الفَتْحِ مِنْ كُدَى	خَرَجَ أَوْفَى الرَّاكِبِينَ بَيْنَ أَغْصَانِ السَّحَاءِ
عِنْدَ خَوْضِ الوَاقِعَاتِ تَرَى مُصَابَرَةَ الفَتَى	هَلْ لَنَا حَالُ الجَسُورِ أَمْ لَنَا خَوْفُ الدِّمَاءِ
مَنْ لِحُسْنِ البَدِيعِ وَمَنْ لِنَجْلَةِ المُرْتَضَى	مَنْ لِأَحْمَدِ الشَّفِيعِ مَنْ لِأَوْلَادِ الكِسَاءِ
نَحْنُ مَفْخَرُ الكِرَامِ وَجُنْدُ الرُّشْدِ وَالتُّقَى	مَا لَنَا تَرْكُ الوَفَاءِ لِلصِّغَارِ وَالنِّسَاءِ
جَاءَ جَيْشٌ لِلنِّضَالِ فَطَابَ عَيْشٌ لِلفَتَى	فِي رِجَالٍ كَجِبَالٍ مَا لَهُمْ خَوْفُ العِدَاءِ
قَدْ أَتَيْنَا فَارِحِينَ لِقُرْبِ المَوْتِ وَالرَّدَى	اُنْظُرُوا يَاعَاشِقُونَ لِأَنْصَارِ الاِصْطِفَاءِ
جُنْدُ الآلِ كَاللَّآلِي وَنَصْرُهُمْ كَنْزُ المُنَى	فَالغِنِيُّ بِالوَلَاءِ فِي الرَّخَاءِ وَالحَبَاءِ

22

Muslim ibn Aqil

Tune: Scottish traditional

Mawlāya ayyid āla Aḥmad   safīnat al-najā
Mawlāya ayyid āla Aḥmad   wa-man bihim najā

1.
And Ibn Aqīl al-Hāshimī
The cousin to our Imam
Was told can you take this message from me
To our brethren in Islam?

2.
Their trustworthy tongues have called me to them
A father for orphaned hearts
A hero they need, a son of Hashem
Who light from shadow parts.

3.
So Ibn Aqīl rode straight to Kufa
By desolate desert hills
He feared neither tyrant nor traducer
The people showed goodwill.

4.
They promised him all would stand beside him,
To fear no Damascus blade,
But Ibn Ziyād was sent to find him,
In a veil of black brocade.

5.

Those multitudes thronged the streets to greet him,
Thinking him their imam,
But heralds proclaimed, behold, obey him,
Here is Syria's steely arm.

6.

So Ibn Aqīl did hide with Hānī
Urwa's pure faithful son,
But Ibn Ziyād was cruel and canny
And fate may none outrun.

7.

Though Ibn Aqīl well plied his sabre,
True martyrdom's crown he won,
He cried to all Kufa, friend and neighbour,
But answer came there none.

CHAPTER 9

Imam Husayn Arrives at Karbala
and Fights the Enemy

The Noble Thane

در رسیدن امام حسین رضی الله عنه به کربلا

Tune: Twa Corbies
Arr. Habib Dunne

plain the mas-ter of the mar-tyr train The knight of light the bold Hus-sein - o with the sword and the sand and the an - gels twain - o with the sword and the sand and the an - gels twain

2

Oh hear my tale, my noble thane
Let me amain your time detain
Help me unwind my tangled skein-o
With the sword and the sand and the angels twain

He stood on Karbala the plain
The master of the martyr train
The knight of light, the bold Hussein-o
With the sword and the sand and the angels twain

Since age of Abel and of Cain
The strife of Godly and profane
The war to whelm the devil's reign-o
With the sword and the sand and the angels twain

The foeman feigns his deep disdain
He fears what Heaven might ordain
For falsehood's fortunes ever wane-o
With the sword and the sand and the angels twain

Our noble hero fears no chain
No desert heat and cruel terrain
Of Heaven's foes he is the bane-o
With the sword and the sand and the angels twain

Afore the host stood al-Hussein
The arrows falling round like rain
His loved ones died with bloody stain-o
With the sword and the sand and the angels twain

So bitterly did Fate ordain
His noblest folk for to be slain
Those of the Cloak, let none disdain! -o
With the sword and the sand and the angels twain

With russet wine in ev'ry vein
Their banners lastly shall attain
The victory and right retain-o
With the sword and the sand and the angels twain

With righteousness from sin abstain
You stand on Karbala the plain
Each faithful heart may heaven gain-o
With the sword and the sand and the angels twain

Events after Karbala

The Field of Misfortune

The Field of Misfortune

Upon the field of misfortune
All my people lie
Their ruddy wounds all untended
Open to the sky.

The devil's blade has been fashioned
In the blaze of hate,
Its poison spirit impassioned
In its fiery fate.

The edge knows thirst that is rabid
Questing here its point
To holy flesh for its scabbard
Blood it shall anoint.

The rainless airs of the valley
Hear my lonely cry
The widowed daughters of Ali
Teach the dust to sigh.

Behold Abbas, hero regal
Hear Sakina's thirst
Father of grace of the eagle
place that maiden first.

To see the blood of my brothers
dye the sorry sands
to hear the keening of mothers
cheeks clenched in their hands.

So teach the ways of fair patience
To the weak and wronged.
Strengthen with hope and forbearance
wretchedness prolonged.

Finale

Ziya Paşa, *Terkib-bend*, Fourth Extract

He changeth morn to even and He turneth night to day;
He maketh summer winter just as He maketh autumn May.
He turns the clay to man, He turns the body back to clay.

For Ibrahim His might transformed the Fire to cooling ray.
For Musa did His wisdom supernal Light as Fire display.
For Musa did His wisdom Light as burning Fire display.

For dole of love He made Ferhad, Mejnun distracted stray.
Showing the Layla-beauty sweet as Shirin before his gaze,
For some fond hope He makes a soul for years to thole dismay.

A body in all luxury He causes long to stay
And then at last He yields it up, up to the clutch of death as prey;
And in the dust sepulchral at the end He doth him lay.

Ziya, the sage is he who doth his helplessness confess
And taketh warning by the things that ever pass before him aye,
And taketh warning by the things that pass before him aye.

Throughout His Kingdom ever rules the Truth e'en as He may;
The universe, e'en as He please, He makes anew or doth away;
The universe, e'en as He please, He makes or doth away.

(Chorus)

Salli rabbi ala'l-nabi amin il-alamayn
muballighi'r-risala, rafa'a qadra'l-haramayn
Salli rabbi wa-sallim ala jaddi'l-hasanayn

Imam al-Haddad, '*Imamun Minna*'.

من ديوان الامام الحداد رضي الله عنه

وَمِنَّا إِمَامٌ حَانَ حِينُ خُرُوجِهِ   يَقُومُ بِأَمْرِ اللهِ خَيْرَ قِيَامِ

فَيَمْلَؤُهَا بِالحَقِّ وَالعَدْلِ وَالهُدَى   كَمَا مُلِئَتْ جَوْرًا بِظُلْمِ طَغَامِ

إِذَا قَامَ قُمْنَا وَالمُوَفِّقُ رَبُّنَا   بِنُصْرَتِهِ إِنْ رَاثَ حِينَ حَمَامِ

وَإِلاَّ فَنَرْجُو أَنْ يَقُومَ بِنَصْرِهِ   فُرُوعٌ مِنَ البَيْتِ المَصُونِ نَوَامِي

وَللهِ رَبِّيَ الحَمْدُ وَالشُّكْرُ وَالثَّنَا   عَلَى نِعَمٍ مَشْكُورَةٍ بِدَوَامِ

وَنَسْأَلُ مَوْلَانَا تَبَارَكَ اسْمُهُ   ثَبَاتًا وَتَأْيِيدًا وَحُسْنَ خِتَامِ

وَتَمَّتْ وَصَلَّى اللهُ أَزْكَى صَلَاتِهِ   عَلَى أَحْمَدٍ مَاانْهَلَّ وَدْقُ غَمَامِ

وَمَا غَرَّدَتْ وُرْقٌ عَلَى غُصْنِ دَوْحَةٍ   وَمَا لَاحَ بَرْقُ النَّجدِ جُنْحَ ظَلَامِ

وَآلٍ وَأَصْحَابٍ وَمَنْ كَانَ تَابِعًا   عَلَى البِرِّ وَالتَّقْوَى وَحِفْظِ ذِمَامِ

32

Tasbih Ashura

تسبيح يوم عاشوراء

سُبْحَانَ الله مِلْءَ الميزَانِ وَمُنْتَهَى العِلْمِ وَمَبْلَغَ الرِّضى وزِنَةَ العَرْشِ لا مَلْجَأَ وَلا
مَنْجى مِنَ اللَّهِ إِلَّا إِلَيْهِ ، سُبْحَانَ اللهِ عَدَدَ الشَّفْعِ والوِتْرِ وَعَدَدَ مَا كَلِمَاتِ اللهِ
التَّامَّاتِ كُلِّهَا ، نَسْأَلُكَ السَّلامَةَ بِرَحْمَتِكَ يَا أَرْحَمَ الرَّاحِمِين وَهُوَ حَسْبُنَا وَنِعْمَ
الوَكِيلُ نِعْمَ المَوْلَى وَنِعْمَ النَّصِيرِ وَلا حَوْلَ وَلا قُوَّةَ إِلَّا بِالله العَلِيِّ العَظِيمِ ، وَصَلَّى
اللهُ تَعَالَى عَلَى سَيِّدِنَا مُحَمَّدٍ وَعَلَى آلِهِ وَصَحْبِهِ وَعَلَى المُؤْمِنِينَ وَالمُؤْمِنَاتِ
وَالمُسْلِمِينَ وَالمُسْلِمَاتِ عَدَدَ ذَرَّاتِ الوُجُودِ وَعَدَدَ مَعْلُومَاتِ اللهِ
وَالحَمْدُ لله رَبِّ العَالَمِين